Kenny Smith

by Mark Stewart

ACKNOWLEDGMENTS
The editors wish to thank Kenny Smith for his cooperation in preparing this book.
Thanks also to Integrated Sports International for their assistance.

PHOTO CREDITS
All photos courtesy AP/Wide World Photos, Inc. except the following:

Rich Kane/Sports Chrome – Cover, 5 center right, 40
University of North Carolina – 4 top left, 14, 15 bottom, 22 top, 39 bottom
Mark Stewart – 48

STAFF
Project Coordinator: John Sammis, Cronopio Publishing
Series Design Concept: The Sloan Group
Design and Electronic Page Makeup: Jaffe Enterprises, and
        Digital Communications Services, Inc.

LIBRARY OF CONGRESS CATALOGING-IN-PUBLICATION DATA
Stewart, Mark.
    Kenny Smith / by Mark Stewart.
        p. cm. – (Grolier all-pro biographies)
    Includes index.
    Summary: Traces the basketball career of the point guard who starred at the University of
North Carolina and then helped the Houston Rockets win their first NBA championship in
1994.
        ISBN 0-516-20174-3 (lib. binding) – 0-516-26022-7 (pbk.)
    1. Smith, Kenny, 1965-   –Juvenile literature. 2. Basketball players–United States–
Biography–Juvenile literature. [1. Smith, Kenny, 1965-   . 2. Basketball players.
3. Afro-Americans–Biography]
I. Title. II. Series.
GV884.S55S84 1996
796.323'092–dc20
(B)   96-21881
                                                                                      CIP
                                                                                       AC

Grolier **ALL-PRO** Biographies™

Kenny Smith

by
Mark Stewart

CHILDREN'S PRESS®
A Division of Grolier Publishing
New York • London • Hong Kong • Sydney
Danbury, Connecticut

Contents

Who

Am I?

There are not a lot of people my age who can say that they have been doing the same thing, day in and day out, since they were six or seven years old. But from the moment I got into my first basketball game, I knew there was only one position I wanted to play: point guard. And there was only one goal I wanted to achieve: a world championship. My name is Kenny Smith, and this is my story . . . "

"From the moment I got into my first basketball game, I knew there was only one position I wanted to play: point guard."

Growing Up

When Kenny Smith was six years old, he had a dilemma. He knew he was good enough to play basketball with the older boys, but the nearest basketball court to the apartment building where he lived was too far away. Kenny and his brother, Vince, came up with a clever solution. They removed the rim from an old, rusted garbage can and nailed it to a telephone pole. After a couple of years practicing on this makeshift court, Kenny was old enough, and good enough, to take his game to the local playgrounds in the Jamaica section of Queens, New York. There he often played with boys who were 12 and 13. Although Kenny was smaller than they were, he could dribble and pass better than any of his teammates, so they were happy to let him play. In fact, they usually allowed him to bring the ball upcourt and run the team.

Kenny got his first taste of organized basketball in the Police Athletic League. He was a great little player who understood the importance of listening to his coach. On one occasion, Kenny listened a little too closely. In the closing moments of a game, Coach Wilmot Benjamin ordered him to "sit on the ball." Kenny did not understand that this meant he should dribble until the clock ran out. Instead he did just as he was told, and actually sat on the ball. The whole gymnasium erupted in laughter, and although Kenny's team won the game it was the most embarrassing moment of his life. Coach Benjamin told him to forget it—he was just happy to have a player who followed his instructions!

As a child and as a pro, Kenny could always pass and dribble better than bigger players.

Kenny was indeed a good listener. When he attended clinics given by NBA stars Walt Frazier and Nate Archibald, he hung on their every word. And in school, he paid close attention to the teacher and asked plenty of questions. Kenny's favorite subject was math. He liked the idea that when a problem did not have an easy answer, you could work it out step-by-step until you found the solution.

He also enjoyed English class. Kenny loved to read, and his favorite book was *A Hero Ain't Nothin' But a Sandwich*. Kenny remembers. "It was a story by Alice Childress about a 13-year-old boy named Benjie who becomes a heroin addict. It was told by all the people who knew him. It was very sad, and it made a huge impact on me. It was about the same time that I began to

Walt Frazier

Nate Archibald

understand how important reading is. Reading is how you obtain knowledge, and knowledge is power. If you don't sharpen your reading skills now, you run the risk of feeling powerless for the rest of your life."

From grade school through high school, Kenny tried to spend the same amount of time reading or studying as he did shooting and dribbling. He knew that his basketball skills would open up opportunities, but he also knew he would have to be smart enough to take full advantage of those opportunities. Kenny had seen a lot of teenagers leave his neighborhood with college scholarships, only to return in disgrace after flunking out. He vowed not to be one of those players. "Two hours playing, two hours working, that was the rule," Kenny says. "Staying disciplined was important for me. I found that being disciplined in one area—sports, for example—helped me stay disciplined in another, such as homework. Of course, the reverse is true. If you're undisciplined in one thing, you'll probably be undisciplined in other things. Staying focused on sports and school also helped me recognize and avoid many of the dangers that existed where I was growing up. I was exposed to drugs and stuff but I never saw it do anything good for anybody. Drugs and alcohol just mess kids up."

Kenny was by no means a "natural" player. He had to work very hard on his shooting because he lacked the size and strength to consistently make long jumpers. To compensate, Kenny developed a shooting motion that looked awkward but helped him throw the ball toward the basket. Although his body eventually filled out, Kenny never changed his shooting style and still uses it today in the NBA.

By the time Kenny reached high school, he was one of the top players in New York. He attended Archbishop Molloy High School, which boasted a great team. He was the team's leader, always raising the level of his game when the Stanners most needed it. Kenny was not the only hot point guard in the city, however. In Brooklyn, Mark Jackson was working

Kenny uses the style he learned as a kid to launch the ball toward the basket.

Mark Jackson

his magic for Bishop Loughlin High School. Kenny and Mark had met years earlier when they played in the same youth league. They soon became fast friends—and rivals. Their battles when Molloy and Loughlin faced each other were legendary, as were their frequent summer-league match-ups and games of one-on-one.

During his senior year, many colleges attempted to recruit Kenny. Eventually, he narrowed his choice down to two schools: the University of Virginia and the University of North Carolina. Virginia's assistant coach had graduated from Archbishop Molloy himself, and he offered Kenny a guarantee that he would start immediately for the rebuilding Cavaliers. UNC could make no such promises because Carolina already had a dominant team led by guard Michael Jordan. In the end, Kenny decided to accept a scholarship from North Carolina. He knew the Tar Heels would be good for all four seasons he spent there, and he thought he had a great chance to win the starting point guard job in his freshman year.

College

When Kenny Smith arrived at the University of North Carolina, only four freshman in history had opened the season in a starting role for the Tar Heels basketball team. Kenny aimed to be the fifth. He worked hard all summer and fall to sharpen his ballhandling, passing, shooting, and stamina. The hard work paid off when Coach Dean Smith named him the number-one point guard.

The team Kenny joined was one of the best ever assembled in college basketball history. Along with Jordan, it starred future NBA stars Brad Daugherty and Sam Perkins. This group got off to a 17–0 start in the 1983–84 season. Kenny shot nearly 60 percent from the floor, and his incredible running speed earned him his nickname, "The Jet."

Kenny became only the fifth freshman to start for the North Carolina Tar Heels.

Years

Kenny's great freshman season, however, was marred when he broke his wrist, missed eight games, and was ineffective after trying to come back too soon. The team finished with a respectable 28–3 record, but they lost to Indiana in the NCAA Tournament. In 1984–85, Michael Jordan had left for the NBA, and Kenny became Carolina's best backcourt player. He improved in all areas, particularly on defense.

Kenny enjoyed a fine junior season, leading the Tar Heels to 28 wins. That summer he was selected to play for the

Kenny's ability to bring the ball upcourt and go to a hoop helped make North Carolina one of the best teams in the country.

15

U.S. national team at the World Championships of Basketball. He joined college stars Muggsy Bogues and David Robinson to give Team U.S.A. an awesome defensive squad. But it was Kenny's offense that turned out to be the difference in the tournament, as he scored 23 points in the gold-medal game. With just 20 seconds left, he hit a clutch shot to seal an 87–85 win and send the Soviet team to its first defeat ever in the World Championships.

Coming home with a gold medal in international competition was important to Kenny. It sent a message to the fans who had followed him since he had been playing in the schoolyards of New York. "I had realized for a while that people looked up to me," he says. "Even back in grade school, I knew it was important to set an example and do the right thing. The gold medal was a symbol of my hard work and discipline and, hopefully, it made kids realize that they could achieve great things, too."

Kenny and Coach Dean Smith talk strategy before the 1984 NCAA tournament.

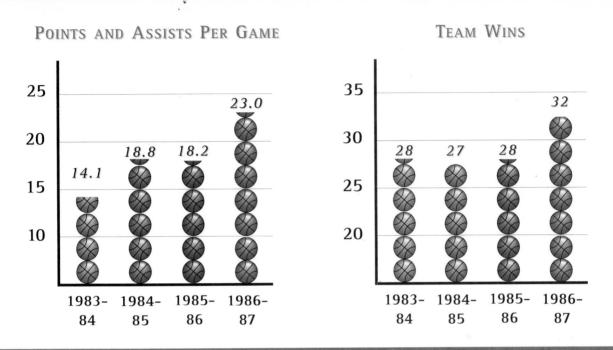

POINTS AND ASSISTS PER GAME

TEAM WINS

Kenny returned to North Carolina for his senior year and led the Tar Heels to a #2 national ranking. He had become a complete player and demonstrated that he could take the ball inside against anyone in the game. A point guard who can both shoot threes and drive the lane is a valuable player, and several NBA teams put Kenny at the top of the lists they were preparing for draft day in 1987. Meanwhile, Kenny was enjoying all of the awards that were coming his way. He was on everyone's All-American team, and *Basketball Times* named him its College Player of the Year.

Road to the

Kenny Smith had played on winning teams his entire life. When his name was called by the Sacramento Kings in the first round of the NBA draft, he knew that he would be starting his professional career with a poor team. Kenny could not imagine how it would feel to lose night after night, but he was willing to do whatever it took to transform his new team into a winner. "The transition from winning nearly every game in college to losing nearly every game in the pros was really tough," Kenny recalls.

On the bright side, Kenny made an interesting discovery about himself and the NBA: the veterans he had admired growing up were not gods. They were flesh and blood, and they had strengths and weaknesses just as he did. When the season started, Kenny was in awe of veterans such as Larry Bird, Alex English, and Moses Malone. By the end of his rookie year, Kenny was confident that he belonged in their company.

Championship

Kenny led the Kings in points, assists, and steals during his second season, but the team kept struggling. The losing continued in his third year with Sacramento, but 46 games into the 1989–90 campaign he got a break when the Kings traded him to the Atlanta Hawks, who then traded him to the Houston Rockets just prior to the 1990–91 season. The Rockets had one of the game's top centers, Hakeem Olajuwon, and two sharp-shooting guards, Vernon Maxwell and Sleepy Floyd. Rounding out the team was power forward Otis Thorpe, who had been Kenny's teammate with the Kings.

In his second NBA season, Kenny led the Kings in points, assists, and steals.

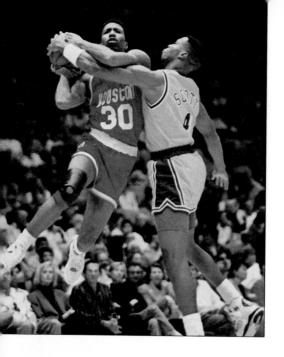

Kenny leads the Rockets over Los Angeles for one of Houston's 52 victories in 1991.

With Kenny at the helm, the Rockets won a team-record 52 games, and coach Don Chaney credited Kenny with making the difference.

By the start of the 1993–94 season, Kenny and the Rockets were ready to establish themselves as one of the NBA's elite teams. The year began with a record-setting 15-game winning streak, and after 23 games Houston was 22–1. They cruised into the playoffs, wiping out the Portland Trailblazers and then erasing a 3–1 deficit to score a dramatic victory over the Phoenix Suns. In the Western Conference Finals, the Rockets faced the Utah Jazz. In the first game of the series, Kenny hit six three-pointers to set a new team mark and got the Rockets rolling to a five-game victory. In the NBA Finals, Kenny returned home as the Rockets faced the New York Knicks. He struggled early in the series but came back to nail a key three-point shot in Game 6. In Game 7, Kenny's teammates looked to him for leadership, and he delivered. He hit his first four shots to breathe life into his exhausted team. The Rockets left the court that night with the first NBA championship in team history.

Kenny piloted the Houston Rockets to NBA championships
in 1994 (left) and 1995 (right).

One of the toughest things to do in pro sports is repeat as league champion. But Kenny and the Rockets were up to the task again in 1994–95. The Rockets made the Finals once again, this time against the Orlando Magic. In Game 1, the Magic built a 20-point lead in the first half, but Kenny got the Rockets back into it with 20 second-half points. Then he sent the game into overtime with a dramatic three-pointer—his seventh of the game! Houston went on to win Game 1 and used that momentum to sweep Orlando. On June 14, 1995, Kenny became the proud owner of a second straight championship ring.

Timeline

1989: Leads Sacramento Kings in points, assists, and steals in second NBA season

1987: Earns All-America honors at North Carolina

1994: Hits 44.7% of three-point attempts during play-offs to help Rockets win NBA title

1990: Traded to Houston Rockets

1995: Helps Rockets win second straight NBA championship

Game

Kenny Smith has been the best player on a losing team and a valuable role player on a championship squad. "I'll take the championship anytime."

Kenny is not only one of the quickest players in the NBA, he is one of the league's best leapers and top shooters. He was the first player ever to compete in the NBA's Slam Dunk Contest and the Long Distance Shootout on the same night.

Kenny concentrates on passing the ball when he is playing the point, but he will not skip an open jumper. "This league is about open shots. That's what it comes down to."

Action!

Kenny doesn't always look to shoot, but if the opening is there, he'll take it.

Kenny likes the responsibility of controlling his team's offense. "When you play the point, it's always your team. You're an extension of the coach on the court."

Kenny says the toughest thing about joining the Sacramento Kings was not the long NBA schedule, but the losing. In college, he lost only 22 games in four years!

Kenny has worn number 30 at nearly every stop of his high school, college, and pro career. During his 33 games with the Atlanta Hawks in 1990, he wore 31 because 30 was already taken.

Kenny's 768 assists at North Carolina are still a school record.

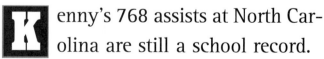

Kenny and teammate Hakeem Olajuwon (left) shut down the lane.

Kenny is one of basketball's most durable players. Only once has he missed more than four games in a season.

What drives Kenny Smith? "Trying to get better. . . . I'm my own toughest critic. It's hard for me to tell myself I've had a good game."

Dealing

After the Rockets lost three of their first four games to the Phoenix Suns during the 1995 NBA playoffs, most people—including a few of Kenny Smith's teammates—thought there was no way they could come back. That is when Kenny stepped forward and demonstrated his leadership.

Kenny remembers, "The papers said it had been 27 years since a team came back from a 3-1 deficit to win a Game 7 on the road, which is what we had to do. But I told the guys I didn't think the damage was irreversible. I said that this was where our professionalism would have to come into play. We took it one game at a time and played three great games to defeat the Suns. After that, we took eight of our next ten games to win the NBA championship!"

With It

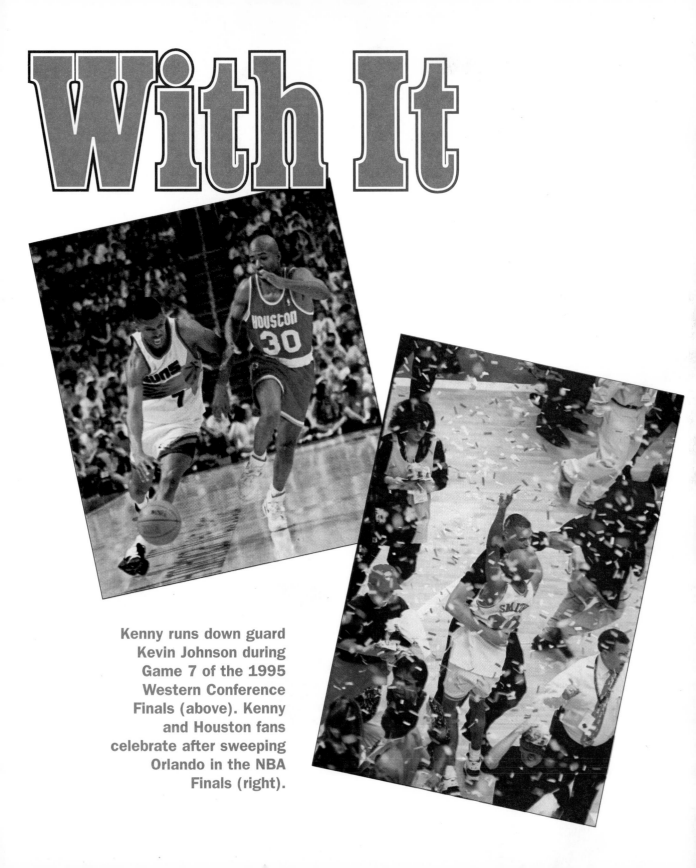

Kenny runs down guard Kevin Johnson during Game 7 of the 1995 Western Conference Finals (above). Kenny and Houston fans celebrate after sweeping Orlando in the NBA Finals (right).

HOW DOES

Kenny Smith is most effective when he is penetrating the defense, drawing double-teams, and then passing to open teammates. To get past his man, however, Kenny must draw him close on defense.

"Actually, my outside shot is the key. If an opponent respects my ability to score from 20 feet, he has to come out and guard me tight. And that opens up all kinds of opportunities around the basket."

Kenny lets a defender get close, then drives by him.

He Do It?

The Grind

The on-court pressures faced by NBA players are among the most demanding in all of sports. For Kenny Smith, however, the off-court pressures can be just as tough. He believes that a player must care about more than wins, losses, and stats.

"A professional athlete carries a lot of responsibility. For me, it's the responsibility of taking care of myself and doing what's right for my family and my career. But it's also being responsible for my teammates, my team, and even the city I'm playing in."

Kenny takes time to talk to a Knicks fan before a playoff game.

Kenny explains to the media his three-point shot that beat the Knicks in the NBA Finals.

Family

Kenny and Dawn Smith have a daughter, Kayla, and were expecting another child in 1996. Family is important to Kenny, whose parents always gave him plenty of love and support. His mother, Annie, and his father, William, always made time to see their son play, trudging through the snow to remote gymnasiums in the winter and sweating it out at sweltering playgrounds to watch Kenny during summer tournaments. The Smiths now own a flower shop in Brooklyn, and they never miss Kenny when his team comes to play the New York Knicks at Madison Square Garden.

Kenny says, "I have a very close family. My father was an engineer and my mother was a schoolteacher. I also have two sisters and my brother, Vince, who I always looked up to as a leader. Everyone in the family was always very supportive of my basketball, which gave me tremendous confidence and made me feel great about myself."

Matters

Wherever Kenny goes, he stays in touch with family. Here he sits with his nephew, Joseph Dawkins, during an interview.

Say What?

Here's what basketball people are saying about Kenny Smith:

"Kenny has great open-court skill and quickness."

—Jerry Reynolds,
  Kenny's coach on Sacramento Kings

"He's our best shooter. We need him on the floor."

—Hakeem Olajuwon, teammate

"Kenny is one of the most competitive people I've ever played against."

—*Sam Cassell, teammate*

"He's an outstanding player, the fastest guy I've ever played against."

—*Mark Jackson, Indiana Pacers guard*

"It's uncanny how he makes the right decision on the break."

—*Dean Smith,*
 University of North Carolina coach

Career

When Kenny Smith came into the NBA, most experts thought he would average 20 points a game playing great ball for a mediocre team. As things worked out, he became a valuable part of one of history's great teams. No, he is not the star. But when the Rockets need a clutch shot or want to change the tempo of a game, Kenny often is the man they turn to. Although he has never averaged 20 a game or made the All-Star team, he has distinguished himself as only the twelfth guard in NBA history to start for back-to-back champions. Nine of the men who share this honor are either in the Hall of Fame or well on their way.

Highlights

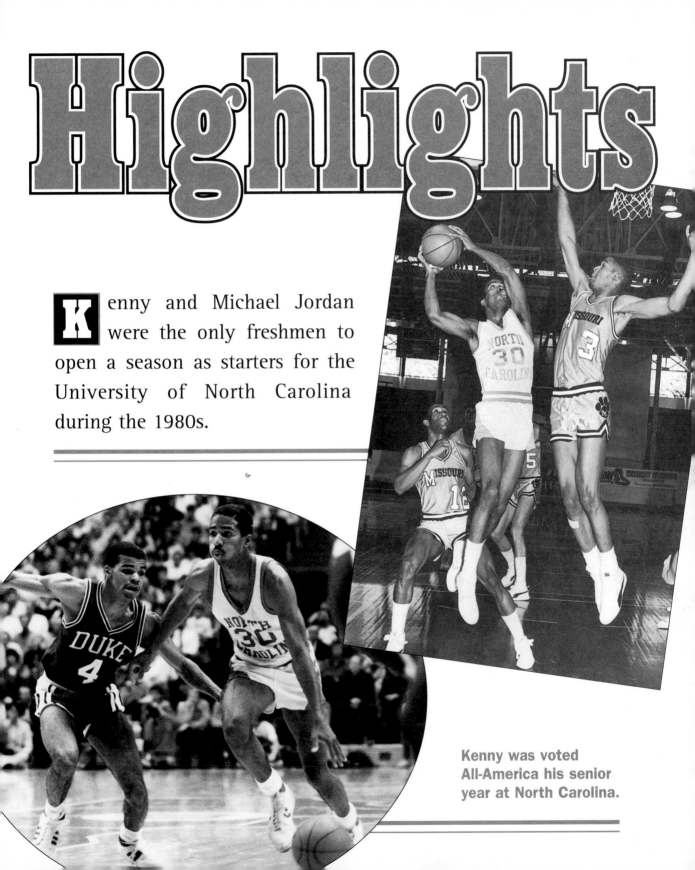

Kenny and Michael Jordan were the only freshmen to open a season as starters for the University of North Carolina during the 1980s.

Kenny was voted All-America his senior year at North Carolina.

Kenny's 768 career assists broke the North Carolina record set by Phil Ford.

The most points Kenny has scored in a game is 41. In college, he did it against Clemson. In the NBA, he did it against the Lakers.

Kenny's layup with 15 seconds left against the Soviet Union gave the U.S. the gold medal in the 1986 World Championships of Basketball.

Kenny was named All-ACC in 1987. He made the NBA All-Rookie team a year later.

Kenny is the Rockets' all-time leader in three-point field goal percentage.

enny led the Kings in points, assists, and steals in just his second NBA season.

enny shot at an amazing 52.0 percent clip during the 1992–93 season. No guard in the NBA was more accurate that year.

enny set an NBA Finals record with seven three-pointers against the Orlando Magic in 1995.

Reaching

When it comes to getting involved with kids, Kenny Smith is one of the most caring, generous people in the game. He regularly gives up his off-days to conduct clinics. He does this because he remembers how deeply he was influenced by NBA legends Walt Frazier and Nate Archibald when he attended their clinics as a child.

Kenny is a big booster of the Aim High Foundation. He also has been an active member of the Big Brothers/Big Sisters organization since his rookie year in the NBA. "When I think back on the relationship I had with my older brother—how he helped me with everything and supported me in anything I was interested in—I felt Big Brothers/Big Sisters was a good way to do the same thing."

Out

Kenny (standing, left) is in New York City to play in the New York All-Star Basketball Classic to benefit Wheelchair Charities.

Numbers

Name: Kenneth Smith Height: 6' 3" Weight: 170 lbs.

Nickname: "The Jet" Uniform Number: 30

Born: March 8, 1965 College: University of North Carolina

Season	Team	FG %	FT %	3 point %	Assists Per Game	Points per Game
1987-88	Sacramento Kings	.477	.819	.308	7.1	13.8
1988-89	Sacramento Kings	.462	.737	.359	7.7	17.3
1989-90	Kings/Atlanta Hawks	.466	.821	.313	5.6	11.9
1990-91	Houston Rockets	.520	.844	.363	7.1	17.7
1991-92	Houston Rockets	.475	.866	.394	6.9	14.0
1992-93	Houston Rockets	.520	.878	.438	5.4	13.0
1993-94	Houston Rockets	.480	.871	.405	4.2	11.6
1994-95	Houston Rockets	.484	.851	.429	4.0	10.4
1995-96	Houston Rockets	.433	.821	.382	3.6	8.5
Totals		.482	.828	.395	5.7	13.2

What If...

I have had a couple of serious injuries in my career, but thankfully, I recovered completely each time. Had I been forced to give up basketball, I think I would have gone one of three ways. My degree in industrial relations would have qualified me to pursue a corporate career. At the same time, I was always into music, so I might have gone into record producing. If I had to choose one career outside of basketball, though, it would have to be investments. I could definitely see myself as an investment broker. I like to analyze situations, and I think my business instincts are pretty good."

Glossary

CATAPULT throw; sling; hurtle

CONSECUTIVE several events that follow one after another

DEFICIT disadvantage; shortage

DILEMMA a situation in which one must make a difficult decision

DURABLE long lasting in spite of much use and wear

STAMINA strength; endurance; staying power

TRANSITION the passage from one stage, activity, or subject to another

UNANIMOUS everyone in agreement

UNCANNY spooky; weird; eerie

VERSATILITY having the ability to excel in many different areas; multitalented

ELITE the best of the best; superior; upper class

MOMENTUM strength or force gained by moving forward

RECRUITED asked to join a team or organization

SCHOLARSHIP money given to a student to help pay for schooling

Index

About The Author

Mark Stewart grew up in New York City in the 1960s and 1970s—when the Mets, Jets, and Knicks all had championship teams. As a child, Mark read everything about sports he could lay his hands on. Today, he is one of the busiest sportswriters around. Since 1990, he has written close to 500 sports stories for kids, including profiles on more than 200 athletes, past and present. A graduate of Duke University, Mark served as senior editor of *Racquet*, a national tennis magazine, and was managing editor of *Super News*, a sporting goods industry newspaper. He is the author of every Grolier All-Pro Biography.